Courageous
FEAR

Courageous FEAR

Michelle (Wimberly) Thigpen

XULON PRESS

Xulon Press
2301 Lucien Way #415
Maitland, FL 32751
407.339.4217
www.xulonpress.com

© 2021 by Michelle (Wimberly) Thigpen

All rights reserved solely by the author. The author guarantees all contents are original and do not infringe upon the legal rights of any other person or work. No part of this book may be reproduced in any form without the permission of the author. The views expressed in this book are not necessarily those of the publisher.

Unless otherwise indicated, Scripture quotations taken from the Holy Bible, New International Version (NIV). Copyright © 1973, 1978, 1984, 2011 by Biblica, Inc.™. Used by permission. All rights reserved.

Printed in the United States of America.

Paperback ISBN-13: 978-1-66281-270-5
Ebook ISBN-13: 978-1-66281-271-2

Table of Contents

Special Thanks vii
Foreword ix
Introduction xi

Chapter 1: The Battlefield 1
Chapter 2: Leaving your comfort zone 13
Chapter 3: Season of Preparation 31
Chapter 4: Pregnant with Promise 43
Chapter 5: From the floor to the fire 55
Chapter 6: Take this cup 67
Chapter 7: The Promise is greater than the Plot 77
Chapter 8: Closing Prayer 87

About the Author 91

Special Thanks

A SPECIAL THANKS to my wonderful grandbabies Khalia, Kiara, Kendall and Kyree. You cause me to persevere, because my fight, is your future.

To my Sisters, Marguerite and Maureen, we have loved one another through many situations.

To my Spiritual Parents Apostle Leroy Washington/ Prophetess Lila Washington who have taught me how to do battle through the Word of God.

To my daughter Glenelle. Your love for me is priceless. You have witnessed the pains and the gains, the weaknesses and the strengths.

And last, but certainly first in my life, to my wonderful husband Bishop George Thigpen. Thank you for believing in me and supporting the ministry in me. You made this happen for me and I will forever love you!

Foreword

COURAGEOUS FEAR IS so fitting a title of Michelle Thigpen's second book. As her younger sister, I have witnessed firsthand Ms. Thigpen's walk from fear to unshakable faith in the power of God! Her humble beginnings have blossomed into a phenomenal testimony of God's grace working in her life.

We can all relate to feeling fearful. Fear can either stifle us and stop us in our tracks, or it can propel us forward. To accomplish the latter, we must allow courage to guide our fears. What would you do if you had no fear of failure? "I would conquer the world," you may say. The reality is, we do live with fear that can limit us and bring our dreams to a screeching halt.

Are you ready to live beyond your fears? Then continue turning these pages and walk with Ms. Thigpen as she takes you on a courageous faith journey! You will laugh and you will cry as she shares her wisdom, humor, and raw feelings. She will take you spiritually from the pit of paralyzing fear to the palace of God's unmerited favor.

Ms. Thigpen is living what she has written within these pages. She will inspire you to dig deep, dare to dream, and dare to live with COURAGEOUS FEAR!

Maureen Palmer

Introduction

I REMEMBER WHEN I first gave my heart to the Lord in March 1993, and the Holy Spirit spoke so clearly to me.

We had a very vivid conversation as if He were sitting in the same room as me. I believe He did that clearly for me because one on my questions was, "are your real?"

I believe for the person who would ask, "can you love as deep as the bible says you can", He would show them love in a very powerful way.

My Pastor, Apostle Leroy Washington said he was intrigued about what took place at Calvary. He explained to his congregation that the Lord took him on a journey to Calvary, and that revelation is so vivid to him. As a matter of fact, whenever he preaches on that encounter, people give their hearts to the Lord. It is as if we are standing at the foot of Calvary. We briefly leave the sanctuary and take a spiritual journey to where our beginnings began.

The Lord truly meets us right where we are with our questions. See for me, I was a very inquisitive child. Little fairy tales did not go over too well with me. When my mother told me about Santa, I had some real serious questions about the perception of one man being able to travel the world and meet every need.

I know I spoiled the whole concept for my mother wanting this to be a magical experience. When I learned the truth about Santa and the tooth fairy, I then began to wonder if one day someone would reveal to me that this Jesus that I was hearing and learning about as a child would one day render a truth that He too indeed does not exist.

Well, the Holy Spirit put that question to rest by showing up the first day that I said, "Lord, come into my life". I have never questioned the authenticity of Jesus. He is as real as real can be!

About a month after I gave my life to the Lord, I was sitting in my sister's living room when I clearly heard the Holy Spirit instruct me to go turn on the computer. I obediently did so. It was then that He told me that my life would be an open book. I then began to write down accounts of my life that had a great impact on me. I stayed up to the wee hours of the morning typing away. I relived every emotion, hurt and pain from the endurance of the events I was writing about. I was emotionally drained by the time I finished writing those accounts.

I did not continue adding more accounts until several months later. I then continued to write about events in my life that were significant. Although the Lord led me to write the accounts instantly after receiving salvation, I did not publish the book 'He Hears Our Prayers' until nineteen years later.

In 2012, He spoke to my spirit and said, "it is time to publish your book".

We are all born with a purpose. Some of us search for a long time to find our purpose. The first time I came to the realization that I was born to die, I felt anger towards my parents for having given birth to me knowing that one day I would have to face death. I thought, 'what is the purpose of this?' Anyone ever have that thought?

That was another question that I had for the Lord. Within the first month, He once again answered me. He said, "your life will become an open book. You have been picked out for such a time as this. Everything that you have encountered that I brought you through was so that you would be a testament to me. Do not be ashamed to tell the deepest things concerning you and what you have lived through. It will not be for shame, but for My glory".

"Out of your obedience, I will bless your coming and your going". I remember falling on my face and uttering, **'purpose'.**

Our greatest purpose in life is to return to the Father. Each of us was put here to make a difference in someone else's life. We come in human form to make a spiritual difference!

I pray right now in the name of Jesus, that before you finish reading this book, that you will undoubtedly know your purpose. You will not let fear interfere with what the Lord will have for you to accomplish in this lifetime, in the name of Jesus.

It takes Courageous Fear to step into your God Ordained Destiny. Come on, let's go!!!

Chapter One

THE BATTLEFIELD

When I was growing up during my high school years, we had a landmark near our school called the Battlefield.

I come from the tough streets of Elizabeth, New Jersey. Our recreational time consisted of having good old fist fights.

Our town was split into three territories: Uptown, Midtown, and Downtown. I was from Uptown. Uptown was where the prominent and want to be prominent lived. It was mainly a Jewish community. During my grammar and middle school days, I went to school with my doctors' and dentists' children. There were approximately (2-3) African Americans in my class that consisted of about 20-25 kids.

My grandmother was a very influential woman and was well respected. There is a park in our hometown named after one of my family members. I must say, I had a good upbringing.

Midtown consisted of African Americans and a lot of Italians. They owned many of the stores on the main street.

Downtown, consisted mostly of African Americans. It was considered the 'tough' part of town. It had two of the roughest projects. There was a suppressed spirit that loomed over that part of town.

Those of us from Uptown only frequent that area if we had family members that resided there, or friends that would have our back!

Until 1977, we had (1) all boy's high school and (1) all girl's high school. They built a new school in 1978 that was co-ed that replaced the other two high schools. Having only that high school meant that everyone (uptown, midtown and downtown) would attend.

The Park called the Battlefield was approximately one mile from the high school. I recently did some research and found that Elizabeth is the home of the battlefields of many pivotal conflicts during the American Revolution.

During my adolescent years, the boys from uptown would always fight the boys from downtown. It was against 'uptown' rules for the girls from uptown to date the boys from 'downtown'.

My girlfriends and I went through a period where we were defying all rules. We decided to date the boys from downtown.

Most of the time our boyfriends would get into fights leaving our area with the boys from uptown.

We all began attending this one high school. I declare there was a fight every day. If you looked at someone the wrong way, the next thing you would hear was, "meet me at the battlefield". By the end of the day, everyone would know who was scheduled to fight at the battlefield.

We did not have school buses, we walked to and from school. My walk from school to home was approximately 1 hour to 1 hour and 15 minutes. Those going downtown walked approximately 1 hour and 30 minutes to 1 hour and 45 minutes.

There was one fight that I will never forget. Two girls were meeting at the battlefield after school to duke it out. Word got around the school. I don't remember the two girls' names; I just know that one was very big for a high-schooler and the other was short and petite. All bets were on the big high schooler. As a matter of fact, folks were feeling sorry for the little petite girl. It was silently determined that she probably had no intentions of showing up.

We did have an escape route from the school you could take if you did not want to fight your scheduled fight, and there are many who would not show up. Some people took "meet me at the battlefield" as a mere invite. By not showing up you were saying "no thank you"!

There would be over 200 of us at the battlefield. We would make a clear circle for the 'fighters' of the hour. The big girl arrived first, confident, and cocky. I will never forget it, here comes the little petite girl, she looked nervous, but she was fully prepared. She had someone to braid her hair and douse her face with Vaseline. She had these big fake gold rings on every finger. The big girl thought she looked very silly and smirked like she had this fight in the bag.

Round 1: They entered their self-created ring, and to everyone's amazement, the petite girl rushes at the big girl with everything in her. She caught her off guard with a hard punch with those big rings and then she snatched the big girls' earrings out her ears and split her earlobes. There was blood everywhere. The big girls' punches were sliding off the petite girls' face. The petite girl scratched the big girls face until she was totally unrecognizable. She had to do that damage by jumping up to reach the big girls' face. There was so much blood running down the big girls' face that she could no longer see her opponent.

The fight is stopped. It is a unanimous decision. The petite girl wins, hands down. I like many others, left the battlefield in awe. I could not get that fight out of my mind. Well, I made several decisions based on that one fight. One, I would never go back to the battlefield again. Two, I would never get into a fist fight and chance ruining my face, earlobes, or confidence.

I realized that day, that the loser of that fight would carry those scars on her face for an exceptionally long time. Her earlobes would be split for a longer time unless she would get them sewn back together.

Honestly, I had nightmares regarding that fight. I kept dreaming of getting beat like that and carrying those scars for the rest of my life. Not that I thought I was this raving beauty, but I did not want to be transformed into a monster.

So, it was then established; no more fighting; use your tongue as a razor; cut deep in an argument and if that does not work, take the escape route if invited to the battlefield.

It worked - no fights during my high school year. There was one girl who continued to provoke me by saying 'stuff' and I truly ignored her. She probably concluded that I had a hearing problem. Hey, whatever works.

You will be surprise that when you are traumatized by an event in your life, what steps you will use to avoid having anything remotely the same ever affecting you like that again.

It may have worked then, but I would learn later in life that you cannot go through this lifetime dodging every battle, especially those that are meant for you to address, and conquer.

I oftentimes look back over my life and can see certain events now from a spiritual perspective.

Don't despise small things or beginnings!

I look at David when the Lord sent Samuel to anoint one of Jesse's sons to become King.

When they came, he looked on Eliab, and said, "Surely the anointed of the Lord is before Him." 7But the Lord said to Samuel, "Do not look on his appearance or on the height of his stature, because I have rejected him. For the Lord sees not as a man sees. For man looks on the outward appearance, but the Lord looks on the heart." 8Then Jesse called Abinadab, and made him pass before Samuel. And he said, "Neither has the Lord chosen this one." 9Then Jesse made Shammah to pass by. And he said, "Neither has the Lord chosen this one." 10So Jesse made seven of his sons pass before Samuel. And Samuel said to Jesse, "The Lord has not chosen these." 11Samuel said to Jesse, "Are these all your young men?" And he said, "There remains yet the youngest, and there he is shepherding the flock." Then Samuel said to Jesse, "Send and bring him, for we will not sit down until he comes here." 12So he sent and brought him in. Now he was ruddy with beautiful eyes and a good appearance. And the Lord said, "Arise, anoint him, for this is he." 13Then Samuel took the horn of oil and anointed him in the midst of his brothers. **And the Spirit of the Lord came on David from that day forward.** *So Samuel arose and went to Ramah.* **1Sam. 16:6-13**

David was not even considered. His family did not realize that while David was out shepherding flock, The Lord was imparting a Shepherd spirit into him. Preparing him to do battle and not fear standing up against giants.

Battles are won based on preparation:

Let us look at David again. He was not afraid to fight against the big Philistine (Goliath):

David said to Saul, "Let no man's heart fall because of him. Your servant will go and fight with this Philistine." 33Saul said to David, "You are not able to go against this Philistine to fight with him. For you are but a youth, and he has been a man of war from his youth." 34David said to Saul, "Your servant was a shepherd for my father's flock, and the lion came and the bear, and took a lamb out of the flock. 35And I went out after him, and struck him, and delivered it out of his mouth. And when he arose against me, I took hold of his beard, struck him, and killed him. 36Your servant slew both the lion and the bear. And this uncircumcised Philistine will be as one of them, because he had reviled the armies of the living God." 37David said, "The Lord who delivered me out of the paw of the lion and out of the paw of the bear, He will deliver me out of the hand of this Philistine." And Saul said to David, "Go, and the Lord be with you." 38Saul clothed David with his armor. And he put a helmet of bronze on his head. He also clothed him with a coat of mail. 39David secured his sword to his armor and tried to walk, but he was not used to it, for he had not tested them. And David said to Saul, "I cannot walk with these, for I have not tested them." So David took them off. 40He took his staff in his hand and chose for himself five smooth stones out of the brook. And he put them in his shepherd's bag, even in a pouch. And his sling was in his hand. Then he drew near to the Philistine. 41 The Philistine came walking and drew near to David, and the man bearing the shield went before him. 42 When the Philistine looked and saw David, he despised him. For he was a youth and ruddy with a handsome appearance. 43 The Philistine said to David, "Am I a dog, that you come to me with sticks?" Then the Philistine cursed David by his gods. 44 The Philistine said to David, "Come to me, and I will give your flesh to the birds of the heavens and to the beasts of the field." 45 Then David said to the Philistine, "You come to me with a sword, a spear, and a shield, but I come to you in the name of the Lord of Hosts, the God of the armies of Israel, whom you have reviled. 46 This day will the Lord deliver you into my hand. And I will strike you down and cut off your head. Then I will give the corpses of the Philistine camp this day to the birds of the air and to the beasts of the earth so that all the earth may know that there is a God in Israel. 47 And then all this assembly will know that it is not by sword and spear that the Lord saves. For the battle belongs to the Lord, and He will give you into our hands." 48 When the Philistine arose and came near to meet David, David hurried and ran toward the battle line to meet the Philistine. 49 David put his hand in his bag and took from there a stone. And he slung it and struck the Philistine in his forehead. Therefore, the stone sunk into his forehead and he fell upon his face to the ground.

50So David prevailed over the Philistine with a sling and with a stone. And he struck down the Philistine and slew him, but there was no sword in the hand of David. **51**Therefore David ran and stood over the Philistine. Then he took his sword and drew it from out of its sheath, and he finished him off and he cut off his head with it. **1Sam. 17:32-51**

Encouraging Word: A life without the Holy Spirit (The Comforter, Guider) can keep us focused on the wrong things. I spent my unsaved life protecting my face from incurring any permanent scarring and all the while my inner man was being scarred to the core.

The enemy wants to scar, damage, and kill our inner man. He knows that is where our purpose/destiny is hidden.

The trick is to put as much focus on the outer portion of our being and let the inner man go completely lacking.

We as Christs' chosen vessels will endure some scars, but they will not damage us and they most certainly will not kill us.

They will not be life threatening scars, but scars of survival. I was so glad that I have been in the same ministry for over 25 years and have been blessed to learn all about spiritual warfare and how to stand on the battlefield and declare the victory in advance.

No longer fearful of what I might encounter, but so hopeful on all that I will attain after my encounters.

The young lady who fought on the battlefield during my high school year, showed up fully equipped. She knew she had a giant to face and she strategically prepared herself. She was not focused on the opponent, but rather on the preparation.

If we prepare by girding ourselves in the Word of the Lord, there is no battle too large for us to live through. The bible says that the battle is not ours, it is the Lords'. We are the vessels to be used to encounter the battle, but it does not belong to us.

David was dressed for battle, so it did not matter what he used to slew Goliath. It says he had a sling and five smooth stones. The stone sunk into his head, not from the force of the sling, but by the force of the Power of the Spirit that was in David.

After Samuel anointed David, it said that the Spirit of the Lord came on David. When David was tending to sheep and protecting them from lions and bears, the Lord was preparing David for the greater battles.

David stood before Goliath with a courageous fear. The Lord embedded him with that while he was shepherding. He prepares us long before we get in the battle. We are then able to look back and see how He was preparing us all along.

It is that same power that allows us to look at the mountain and tell it to be removed. Goliath represents the insurmountable mountains that we face. We have the force in us that operated through the sling. In David's time it was the Lord's spirit. In our time, since Christ left the Comforter, It is the Holy Spirit. It's through the Holy Spirit that we can declare that *"No weapon formed against us shall prosper and every tongue that wags against us shall be condemned.* **(Isa. 54:17)**

Chapter Two

Leaving Your Comfort Zone

I remember when I was living a life of hardship and feeling so defeated. I was deep in sin and could not see my way out. I remember crying out to the Lord and saying, "I know I am not worthy of asking, but could you please consider helping me get out of this pit?"

I had moved my children to Virginia to live with my sister and I would visit every weekend. My plan was to work for six months in New Jersey and then transfer to Virginia. I had to make that commitment to my job to be entitled to a transfer.

I had been on that job for twelve years and was making fairly good money. The benefits were exceptional and at the pace I was going, I would be able to retire by my mid 50's.

I never went to church with my kids, but I would get them ready every Sunday while I was there. Several years prior when I came to Virginia, I went to church and got saved and I accepted Jesus as my personal Lord and Savior. Getting saved did not give me a life-changing experience, but it did seem like it was a good place to start.

I did not stop sinning, but I did not quite feel the same excitement. It did not make me hungry for the Word, but it did make me conscience of what may or may not be pleasing unto God. It opened an awareness in me. It is like a blind man now being able to see some light. Cannot quite make out figures yet but now been exposed to a sense of light.

On Easter weekend 1993 when I visited the children, I decided to go to church that Sunday. I talk about this experience in my book "He Hears Our Prayers". The week prior, my sister returned home from church, singing, "I got the Victory". It seemed like she was singing to the depths of my soul. I fell to my knees and began to cry out to the Lord, to please allow me to sing that song like that. Not hit the notes (I am the worse singer), but to be able to sing from the depths of my soul "Victory" because I have tasted it, sensed it, smelled it, and now it can be an aroma to someone else's soul! That note does not come from your vocal cords, it comes from the heavenly realm!

She was on the first floor and I was in the basement. I was crying out to the Lord, the One who had saved me years prior. This was the beginning of forming a relationship with Him. Not just accepting Him but knowing Him. We accept some friend requests on Facebook from people we do not know. There has never been a formal introduction and no relationship had been established.

When we accept Christ in our life, that is not when the intimacy begins. The acceptance is like a handshake. The intimacy comes when you allow Him to indwell you.

Let's liken it to a virgin that's getting married. The marriage is not considered consummated until the husband breaks through the hymen and the blood trickles down and they become one. He has now entered the place where no other has been.

Christ indwells us when we accept and get filled with His Precious Holy Spirit. The Holy Spirit enters a place where no one has ever been, our inner and secret place. The blood of Jesus now trickles down on us and we become one.

There is a place in us that not even our mate can reach. It is reserved for the Holy Spirit.

Back to the basement floor, I am being touched by the Master and I desire more of His touch. I go upstairs and tell my sister that I will be attending church next Sunday.

I counted down the days, I waited in great expectation. I felt like a lover whose love had gone out to sea and was waiting with bated breath for his return.

Finally, Easter Sunday, and we are on our way to church. The message is on the cross and how He died so that I may live. How he loved me so, that He laid down His life for me. No one has ever loved me so. Then there was an altar call. I only went to the altar one or two times prior. The last time I went to accept Him as my personal Lord and Savior. This time I went running to accept Him in a personal way. There is a difference!

Instantly, I was filled with the Holy Spirit with the evidence of speaking in tongues. Somehow, I knew my life would never be the same.

I instantaneously started viewing things differently. I did not want my boyfriend to touch me any longer. I realized that it was sin, and he had no right to my body. It dawned on me that even though I was separated from my husband of three years, that I was still his wife and I could not have an intimate relationship with another man, it was adultery.

I repented for not knowing. It may seem so obvious, but when blindsided by the enemy, wrong seems right and right seems wrong.

We are tricked into thinking that we can create our self-guiding morals and that is satisfactory. We can convince our self that if we are not murdering anyone, what we decide to do with our bodies is fine. We are blinded and not aware that we are killing ourselves and separating ourselves from the One we originated from. It is the enemies desire that we do not return to the Father.

The following week, I returned to Virginia, excited to get back in the presence of the Lord. I am receiving the Word and feeling a strength in me build up that I have never felt before. I had ended my relationship with the boyfriend. However, when I returned on Sunday night, he called begging me to see him once again. He said he just wanted to talk. He said he just wanted me to take a ride with him. As he is talking about how much he loves me, I can see this vision of him taking his white Bronco and crashing it into a brick wall with me in the car.

As he continues to talk, I am not quite understanding where this vision is coming from. And then I can hear him say, "I just need to see you one more time", that is all I need. It instantly clicked, he wanted to kill me.

I always knew he had an anger problem. He would get upset with me when he was driving and would drive fast. I would always have to calm him down. I could not figure out how a man with such an anger issue could have a high position job in law enforcement and be able to carry a gun.

I dated him for several years without him meeting my children, and my children not meeting him.

Back to the vision. As he is talking, I was able to listen to what was coming out of his spirit and not out of his mouth. This was my first time encountering this type of experience. I stopped him in mid-sentence and said, "Not only will I not meet you, but I know you have every intention on trying to kill me, even if it means taking your life in the interim. This new love I have in my life has the power to show me things that are yet to come." He hung up on me and we never spoke again.

I sat on my bed and wept. I realized that there are scheduled events in our life that the Lord will not allow to happen. These are unseen occurrences and plots that we are shielded from. Then there are seen occurrences; the ones that the Lord allows the Holy Spirit to reveal to us. The Holy Spirit warns. He warned me against the harm that was set before me. The boyfriend hanging up, confirmed the warning.

The next weekend that I visited, it was then that the Holy Spirit told me not to return to New Jersey. I tried to reason and bargain with the Holy Spirit. I explained that even though I had dealt with so many hardships, the one thing I had going for myself was my job of twelve years and all its wonderful benefits. I started working there at nineteen years old. It was my comfort zone. When I could not rely on anyone or anything else, I could rely on my job. It meant the world to me.

I heard the Spirit say, "I have a better plan for you, and I need you to trust Me". I went to my sister and said, "I am not going back to New Jersey". I only had a weekend worth of clothes. While in New Jersey, I was living with my father and stepmom and my furniture was in storage.

I called them and advised them that I would not be returning and when I am instructed, I will come back and pack the stuff in my room. I also called my job and resigned. I apologized for the short notice.

I did not understand the command, but I believed in the Commander. He first instructed me to start writing my book "He Hears Our Prayers". He said start writing about all the hardships you endured. As I began writing about the hardships, it was then that I realized that He was there during every disappointing encounter. It was amazing to me. This is the unseen. The times and situations where we think it is by luck or pure happenstance that we survived or dodged a bullet. During the time of writing that book, I began to fall in love with Christ, because I realized that He loved me way before I knew or loved Him.

This was the first time I went without a job in all my adult life. I had thought if I had any accomplishments up until this point, it was that I took care of myself and my children and did not ask for handouts or had to depend on anyone (not even my husband).

I began attending noon day prayer on a regular. It was that time that I realized just how broken and wounded I was. The accomplishment that vied to be my greatness fiat, was revealed to be the worst thing for me. I did not depend on anyone because I did not trust. That type of independence was my wall against the world. In building that wall, even Christ would have a hard time fully getting in.

So, He had to chisel that away. By doing that, he had to put me in a dependent position. Learn how to depend. I had to depend on my sister and her husband to feed me and my children. I had to depend on them to maintain a roof over our heads.

In the meantime, I am being introduced to joy, peace, love, and patience for the first time in my life. I did not worry about paying bills. I was able to focus on getting my life pieced back together. I will forever be grateful for that time of refuge.

What I left behind, did not pale in comparison as to what I would gain. God's timing is not like our timing. He had me write that book in 1993 and not have it published until 2012. After I sat and wrote all my encounters, I saved the writings on a disk and did not pay it any more attention.

I took some excerpts from the pages I typed and about a year later, I submitted one of the accounts to be used for someone who was publishing a book on testimonies. I thought this must be what the Holy Spirit meant about it being writings for a book and I was fine with that.

The Lord would bless me in 2009 to start a business from nothing. Three years later, He would speak to my heart and say, "it is time to publish the book." I had almost forgot about the book and had to remember where it was saved.

I remember the night I started writing the book and the Lord spoke and said that the calling on my life was to be an open book testimony. He has instructed me to tell things most Christians would not feel comfortable in telling. I agreed that night.

The benefits that he told me to walk away from cannot compare to the benefit plan He had for my life.

Leaving your comfort zone will MAKE you depend on and trust the Lord every step of the way.

Let us look at when Abram left his comfort zone and what He inherited in the process:

Now the Lord said to Abram, "Go from your country, your family, and your father's house to the land that I will show you. 2I will make of you a great nation; I will bless you and make your name great, so that you will be a blessing. 3I will bless them who bless you and curse him who curses you, and in you all families of the earth will be blessed." **Gen. 12:1-3**

When the Lord removes you from your comfort zone, He will give you a glimpse of what He has planned for you. His plan is greater, and it will be for His glory.

You cannot step out of your comfort zone unless you first trust in Him. Then you must do as the scripture states, ***walk by faith and not by sight*** *(2Cor. 5:7)*. This might seem like an easy thing to do, but it is not. I know way too many Christians who still move by what they can naturally see. They move within their own confines. If they have enough money, they will do it. If they have the proper transportation, they will go. If they have enough education, they will pursue the job.

That is not moving in faith, that is living a safe life. I love risk taking Christians. Those seeing beyond their limits. It creates powerful testimonies that can take a dying world by storm. When you see me, I do not want you to see my limits, but I do want to display the limitless abilities of the God I serve.

Look at what the Lord promised Abram. In verse two, He said He would make his name great. His name did not become great overnight. First, the Lord had to change his name to Abraham because that is the name He was referring to. I love the Lord, truly I do.

He did not approach Abram and say, I am going to change your name and then make it great. No, He said, I will make your name great. If the Lord explained to us at the onset all that He planned to do for us and how long the plan would take, most would abort the mission.

He lays out his plan/vision for us and then it is up to us to trust Him and know that His timing is perfect.

He had me write the book at the beginning of my salvation. I did not publish the book until nineteen years later. Why? He knew that this new journey that He set me on would cause me to forget the hardships that I had endured. But the hardships were meant for me to tell somebody, so that they would know that they can get the victory over any situation. When I read the book now from time to time, it feels like I am reading about someone other than myself.

He did not want me to change any of the contents that I had written. I wanted to add some revelation to it. I had now gone through eight years of Theology School. He said 'no'. He wanted that book to be written by a newly saved Christian who had encountered troubling days but was able to look back and see that He never leaves or forsaken. I went to church all my childhood and got baptized. I knew of Him, but now I know Him.

When you leave the comfort zone and begin your journey to fulfil His promise, expect some opposition.

Abraham encountered opposition. As time went on, it began to seem as if the promise was not going to come to pass. Every now and then the Lord would send a reminder that a promise is a promise.

When Abram was ninety-nine years old, the Lord appeared to him and said, "I am Almighty God. Walk before Me and be blameless. 2And I will make My covenant between you and Me and will exceedingly multiply you." 3Abram fell on his face and God said to him, 4As for Me, My covenant is with you, and you shall be the father of a multitude of nations. 5No longer will your name be called Abram, but your name will be Abraham, for I have made you the father of a multitude of nations. 6I will make nations of you, and kings will come from you. 7I will establish My covenant between Me and you and your descendants after you throughout their generations for an everlasting covenant, to be God to you and your descendants after you. 8All the land of Canaan, where you now live as strangers, I will give to you and to your descendants for an everlasting possession, and I will be their God. **Gen. 17:1-8**

What a promise! Have you ever had God promise you something that seemed too far out of your reach to fathom the very idea? He would not speak it to you, if it could not be so. There is a preparation processing period that must first take place. Many Christians lose hope during this duration.

Abraham's wife started losing hope during the preparation period. Let us take a look:

Now Sarai, Abram's wife, had borne him no children, and she had a maidservant, an Egyptian, whose name was Hagar. 2So Sarai said to Abram, "The Lord has prevented me from having children. Please go in to my maid; it may be that I will obtain children through her." Abram listened to Sarai. 3So after Abram had been living for ten years in the land of Canaan, Sarai, his wife, took Hagar her maid, the Egyptian, and have her to her husband Abram to be his wife. 4He went in to Hagar, and she conceived. **Gen. 17:1-8**

Abram was eighty-six years old when Hagar bore Ishmael to Abram. **(Gen. 16:16)**.

Sarai losing hope did not stop the Lord from returning to Abram when he reached ninety-nine years old and reaffirming to him that the promise He presented was still going to come to pass.

We cannot reinvent the wheel of God's promises. We should not become self-making miracle machines. It does not work in that manner. We will cause our promises to be delayed.

Then God said to Abraham, "As for Sarai your wife, you will not call her name Sarai, but her name will be Sarah. 16I will bless her and give you a son by her. I will bless her, and she will be the mother of nations. Kings of peoples will come from her." 17Then Abraham fell on his face and laughed and said in his heart, "Shall a child be born to a man that is a hundred years old? Shall Sarah, who is ninety years old bear a child?" 18Abraham said to God. "Oh, that Ishmael might live before You!" "Then God said, "No, but your wife Sarah will bear you a son, and you will call his name Isaac. I will establish My covenant with him as an everlasting covenant and with his descendants after him. **Gen 17:15-19**

Encouraging Word: Purpose is not birthed overnight. Your greatest blessing will come when You trust the Lord enough to get out of your comfort zone. For some, your comfort zone is your secured job, when the Lord has called for you to be a business owner, and for some, the Lord is beckoning you to do Ministry fulltime.

Seek the Lord and see what you are holding onto and why you are not sure how to fully trust the Lord to replace it with His purpose.

We were born to accomplish the purpose He has placed on our life. Too many people leave this realm never obtaining the destined purpose.

By the world's standards, you may seem remarkably successful, but is it what the Lord has for you? No one can tell you what that is, only the Lord.

He has a way of nudging us and sending confirmation our way. We have a way of ignoring all the signs due to our inner fears.

Just because it feels comfortable, does not make it purpose driven.

When the Lord spoke to me to leave it all behind and follow Him, all sorts of fears came over me. although I was not happy and not at peace, I did not want to leave what was comfortable to me.

I had put myself in position where I did not depend on anyone for anything. My job was like my security blanket.

And now the Lord was telling me to uncover. However, when I uncovered, I realized just how broken I was.

My mind was scattered, my heart was crushed, and my body was bruised. All of that was hidden under the comfort of my security blanket.

He did not want me to trust that my sister and her husband could feed me and my children, He wanted me to trust that wherever He leads me to, He would provide, and He would bless those that bless me.

I had a trust issue. It had been so severely damaged. He knew that and He began to put me in positions where I would have to trust.

He showed me His promise for my life, and I am now stepping into that destiny. It is twenty-five years later, and the journey has been challenging as well as the absolute best journey I have ever taken.

I have done a lot of traveling. Not in this world, but from this realm to the spiritual realm. I take round trips all the time. And when I return to this realm for a moment, I return with more power and more authority. With that power and authority, I can leave my comfort zone on a moment's notice! Go for the vision that has been set before you!

Chapter Three

Season of Preparation

I REMEMBER TELLING my young adult children in 2007 that they had two years to figure out what they wanted to do in life because the Lord had spoken to me in a dream that a major change was coming my way in the next two years.

My son would be eighteen and my daughter would be twenty when the two years approached. Whatever they decided to do I would support them, but we would not reside under the same roof. I told my kids, "as for me and my house, we would serve the Lord". That did not seem like the road they wanted to embrace and after turning eighteen, they would have the right to then move and go for what they desired.

The two years approached us very quickly and the Lord reminded me to start packing. I had no clue where I was headed, I was just being obedient to the Spirit of the Lord.

I started selling my valuables out of my house, big screen tv, exercise equipment, furniture, appliances, etc.

During the time that I started packing, a good friend of mine called and said he was offered an opportunity that he felt was over his head. He said he immediately thought of me for the position.

I was already working and making surprisingly good money, but I decided to entertain the idea he brought to my attention.

A business owner in the Richmond area wanted to expand her business to the Northern Virginia area and needed someone to manage the office for her. Her business was in the healthcare industry and that was the area I had been working in for the last couple of years.

I sat and met with her and she shared her business plan with me. I agreed that I would help her establish her business in this area. She told me to start doing research on the cost of the license and search around for a reasonable office space.

I was still working my full-time job and packing to go wherever God was leading me. Yet, I still found the time to assist her with her requested research.

I am a go-getter; you give me a task and I am on it. I do not procrastinate, I get busy. I love a good challenge.

Within one week I had obtained all the information she had requested. I gave her a call to see if she wanted to meet with me to discuss my findings. She indicated she was not available and for me to set a time to meet with the owner of the building I had located.

I set up an appointment between the owner, her and myself. She did not show for the meeting nor did she give me a call. I made my apologies to the owner. Later that evening, she called and said she had gotten stuck in traffic.

I scheduled a second meeting with the building owner at her request and she was unable to make it to that meeting. I once again apologized to the owner. Later when I spoke to her she said she was in a meeting and was unable to call me to cancel. I told her that I thought the office space was very affordable and it should have enough room for what she needed.

It just so happened that the owner of the office space lived in the Richmond area. I had arranged for him to stop by her office to drop off the lease at her request.

She never called him back, nor did she sign the lease. The next time that she and I spoke, I was in my car driving with a friend who I carpooled with. I had her on speaker phone since I was driving, and she began to yell at me in a very unprofessional manner. I only asked her if she had the opportunity to review the lease and did she need me to do anything else from my end.

That is when she began to yell and say that she will let me know when she reviews the lease. I very politely told her that I don't do business with someone who believes that they have a right to yell at a person who is trying to assist them. I told her thanks but no thanks.

My carpool friend said, "I cannot believe she yelled at you like that", you only presented her with one legitimate question". I said, exactly. Then she proceeded to say, "why can't you open your own home care business? You have years of experience and you were smart enough to research all of the necessary steps in starting the business for her." I immediately responded to my friend by saying, "I don't have money to start a company. I have no idea how to run a business."

I did not entertain that thought in the least bit. A couple of days later, the business owner had her young assistant call me to apologize on her behalf. She said, "she yells at me all the time, I am used to it. She does not mean any harm; she is just extremely high strung." I asked the young lady how old she was, and she said twenty-one. I told her that perhaps at her age she did not mind someone yelling and talking down to her, but at forty-seven, I just was not going to tolerate it.

I had a job and a rather good one. It was not worth it to me to give up my peace just to advance a step further in my career.

A couple of days later, she called me herself. I told her I would not be changing my mind. I explained to her that our personalities would clash. I handle the workforce in a calm and peaceful manner and having someone to raise their voice at me when things get challenging would not work for me. I thanked her for the opportunity but decided to decline.

She kept calling me for quite a while, but I would not answer. My mind was made up. I knew it was not a good fit. I could not work under those conditions.

I decided to meet with the building owner one more time, to apologize in person for wasting his time. He was such a nice gentleman. I let him know that it did not work out with me and the business owner, and perhaps since he dropped off the lease to her in person, he would hear from her. I just wanted him to know that since he met with me face to face on two occasions it was only right for me to extend my apology.

When I was leaving out of the building, I heard a voice say to me, "this space is for you". I honestly ignored the voice.

As I went back to packing my bags unbeknown to me where my next destiny would lead me, I had a sense of joy in my spirit. How can you be packing, having no clear direction, but be full of joy?

Everything pretty much was packed. I had about two more weeks left on my lease. I passed the building every day on my way to and from work. I had this strange feeling that I would be coming in and out of that building in the future.

I kept trying to dismiss the thought because it made no sense to me. Yet I could not shake what I was internally experiencing.

One day, I parked in the parking lot of the building and said, "Holy Spirit, what are you trying to show me?" I agreed with myself that I would schedule a meeting with the owner of the building and ask him to meet with me once again.

I truly was not sure why I had scheduled the meeting. I was truly following the tugging of my heart. When I met with him, the first thing I asked was did he hear back from the business owner from Richmond. He said he did not and that he had left her a couple of messages that went unreturned.

The next thing I blurted out was that I was interested in leasing the office space for myself. I told him I was thinking of starting my own business. Making that declaration came off the top of my head. I told him I thought it would only be fair to give the business owner in Richmond thirty days to respond back to him. He said that two weeks had already passed since his last message and he would give her another two weeks. It just so happened that I had two more weeks left on my lease. Of course, I said, "if this is you Lord, then it will all come together, decent and in order."

Two weeks go by and I am packing up my U-Haul truck. I get a phone call from the building owner. He mentioned that he did not hear back from the business owner and if I was still interested in the space, I could pick up the lease.

I am excited and extremely nervous at the same time. I had limited funds and no business owner experience. Did

I allow my mind to play tricks on me? Was I being set up by the devil?

I immediately went into prayer and said that 'fear is not of God". I thought of Noah when God gave him the command to build the Ark. He did not have all the materials he needed to begin, but He trusted God.

I went to pick up the lease as if I had thousands of dollars in the bank. I confidently told him that I would get the lease back to him by the end of the week.

I had one more week in my house before it was time to hand over the keys. I had brought my sister with me when I picked up the lease. I told her to be in prayer with me that the Lord would order my steps.

The next night I called my sister and said I need a name for the business. We went back and forth on names and then it dawned on me. I would name the business after our mother who had passed away of cancer.

Still no money in my pocket but I am getting so excited about this whole idea of becoming a business owner with a business that would honor my mother for a lifetime.

The vision was greater than the bank account. The spirit revealing of it was mightier than the natural missing links.

It was then that I decided that "Lord, I am going to trust you and not focus on what I do not have."

9 *This is the account of Noah and his family.*

Noah was a righteous man, blameless among the people of his time, and he walked faithfully with God. [10] Noah had three sons: Shem, Ham and Japheth.

[11] Now the earth was corrupt in God's sight and was full of violence. [12] God saw how corrupt the earth had become, for all the people on earth had corrupted their ways. [13] So God said to Noah, "I am going to put an end to all people, for the earth is filled with violence because of them. I am surely going to destroy both them and the earth. [14] So make yourself an ark of cypress wood; make rooms in it and coat it with pitch inside and out. [15] This is how you are to build it: The ark is to be three hundred cubits long, fifty cubits wide and thirty cubits high. [16] Make a roof for it, leaving below the roof an opening one cubit high all around. Put a door in the side of the ark and make lower, middle and upper decks. [17] I am going to bring floodwaters on the earth to destroy all life under the heavens, every creature that has the breath of life in it. Everything on earth will perish. [18] But I will establish

my covenant with you, and you will enter the ark—you and your sons and your wife and your sons' wives with you. [19] *You are to bring into the ark two of all living creatures, male and female, to keep them alive with you.* [20] *Two of every kind of bird, of every kind of animal and of every kind of creature that moves along the ground will come to you to be kept alive.* [21] *You are to take every kind of food that is to be eaten and store it away as food for you and for them."*

[22] *Noah did everything just as God commanded him.* **Gen. 6:9-22**

Encouraging Word: Success does not come without sacrifice! I love the way the Lord establishes our trust in Him. He will advise us to do something that seems foolish. The advisement comes with an option to rely exclusively on Him.

He takes the foolish things to confound the wise. When we step into our next level in Christ, we must do so by laying aside every weight that would easily beset us. That first weight can and usually is our own mindset. We have been conditioned to move within our means. Trusting Christ for the impossible and the unattainable goes beyond our means.

There is nothing miraculous when we stay within the confines of our properties. But if you ever want to experience His miraculous power and see Him beyond this realm, you must step out and trust!

He truly can open doors no man can shut and shut doors no man can open. Noah was given a command with not one piece of material at hand or even nearby. Yet He trusted that the Lord would provide since He spoke the commission into the atmosphere.

Noah had to look beyond his understanding and just rely solely on the spoken word. I know that the Lord has laid on your heart to step out and believe along the course of the way.

You have reserves; you do not feel qualified; you do not have the resources to begin to put into practice the vision or dream that the Lord has given you.

He would not have given you the vision without providing the provision. Just keep in mind that the provision does not show up at the same time of the vision. That is where we get confused. If the provision were available at the onset of the vision, how could your faith be enhanced?

The bible says that 'faith moves the hand of God'. We expect God's hand to be all in our vision minus faith. I am here to tell you, not so.

For all that the Lord blesses us with, it is for His glory, His edification. That kind of glory and edification comes by faith.

Let us see in the next chapter how I fare with this command He gave me, minus the resources!

Chapter Four

PREGNANT WITH PROMISE

I BELIEVE IN the power of prayer. I knew that this new venture would take lots of prayer, faith and trust. I was prepared for the journey.

I mentioned to no one what I was about to embark on. I shared it with my oldest sister because I knew she would be by my side to push and encourage me. I also explained to my children that I was following the voice of the Lord and they should trust my next steps as I trust Christ.

The Lord laid it on my heart to share my vision with my cousin Jimmy. I asked him if he could loan me the first month's rent and the one-month security. He did not hesitate at my request.

I was still working my fulltime job at a Nursing Company, managing, and placing Registered Nurses on assignments.

I had my daughter resign from her job and had her work in the office during the day. It is a requirement for someone to be in the office during regular business hours.

Within one month of establishing the business (which was not yet generating revenue), the Lord spoke to my heart and said, "you must resign from your position for the sake of your integrity". I rebuked whom I assumed was the devil and went to work the next day. There was another tug at my spirit, repeating the same thing.

I immediately went into prayer. I had one week left in my townhouse before I had to move and now the Lord was telling me to leave my comfortable paying job to work fulltime in a business that was yet to generate income.

The Lord was letting me know that there was a conflict with me working with nurses on my job and then having a company that too was hiring nurses. In no way did the Holy Spirit want anyone to think I was working there to gather employees from them.

I gave my two weeks' notice and I vowed to the Lord that I would work the business fulltime. With no money coming in and the closing of my current residence, I then asked the Lord, "where should I reside"? The Lord then instructed me to make a pallet on the floor in my private office space.

When I went fulltime, my daughter was able to get her another job. Both of my adult children had somewhere to stay. It was me and Jesus at the office.

I would work on creating forms and applying for contracts until the wee hours of the morning. Then I would make my pallet on the floor and hold fast to the vision.

There were times when I would cry myself to sleep, I would feel so alone from time to time. Then I would call on the name of Jesus and ask Him for the peace that surpasses all understanding.

I must admit that it was during those times that I would have the absolute best conversations with the Holy Spirit. It was a large office building with other tenants in it. But at night it was just me and the Holy Spirit.

I had my car so I would go to my sister's house to shower. When my adult children got their own apartments, I would switch up and go to their place to shower.

I remember when my car broke down and I took it to the car shop for repair. The shop repaired more than I had requested, so I was unable to pay the bill.

The shop owner said that there was more than one way I could pay for the car, since I did not have the money. If I did not learn anything else by sleeping on that floor, I learned that I could do without material things as long as I had Jesus. My integrity would not be compromised under no circumstance.

I owned my car and had the title to it. I told the shop owner that I would be back. Perhaps he thought I would return and take him up on his offer. Absolutely not! I returned with the title and told him to sell the car and get his money. My car was worth way more than the tab of the bill.

First lesson learned: The Holy Spirit instructed me to have that same integrity as a business owner. I was never to compromise who I am in Christ under no condition. The success of the business would come, by being always honest and Christlike. Do not sell myself short to gain financial wealth.

This business industry is incredibly competitive. I have seen people cut many corners to win. I vowed to the Lord that I would not be one of them. Sleeping on the floor provided me with a humbleness that I cannot describe.

My office suite had a kitchen area, so I had a microwave and a little toaster oven. I really had everything I needed at my disposal. I had a television in my office with cable. I did not spend much time watching it, I stayed in my Word. I was drawing closer to Jesus by the day.

When I shared with my younger sister Maureen that I was residing in my office, she gave me her queen-size blow-up mattress. I felt like I was staying at the Hilton Hotel.

I would walk to the bank to make my deposits since I no longer had a car. My company provided home care and transportation services to the elderly and disabled.

I thought it was ironic that I provided the two services that I did not have for myself. Home care service is provided to those who want to stay in the comfort of their home instead of living in a nursing home.

It made providing those services much more special to me. I knew firsthand how important it was to maintain a home and a means of being transported to significant appointments.

It is during those times in the valley that we can gain much insight and wisdom. The Lord was building purpose in me. I am glad He took me by way of the valley to get me to where He wanted me to be.

He had taught me early on in this, that I was to not ask anyone for shelter and that I was to trust Him wholeheartedly during this time of birthing. He gets all the glory.

I used the teachings from my ministry to apply it to my situation. Our mantra and scripture of reference is that 'we walk by faith and not by sight'.

I was not focused on what I did not have, but on what I was going to obtain. It was such an enlightening spiritual journey for me. I learned how to solely depend on the Lord. I fell more in love with Him at that time. That one-on-one with no interruption was priceless.

All my accomplishments up to this point was done in my own strength. I had to pull on the strength of Jesus to birth this promise. I had to be assured that it was nothing but the grace of God that brought me through.

Because I am writing this nine years later, I know without a shadow of a doubt, it had to be done in this matter. What I would encounter over the next nine years, I could only survive knowing that the 'Lord would never leave nor forsake me'. And when I have no one, He is there. I have pushed beyond some unthinkable situation in this business. I was strengthened to endure all types of hardships, betrayals, set-ups, set backs, back stabbing events by giving birth on that floor nine years ago.

I lived in the office for nine months. Just enough time to push the promise to its purpose.

After the ninth month I found a young Christian woman living in her five bedroom home alone. I rented her fully furnished basement apartment. She and I would stay up many nights talking about the goodness of Jesus.

The Lord provided me with a comfortable place to lay my head after I gave birth to the promise.

Look at Joseph in Genesis. The Lord gave him a vision. He had to give birth to it. It did not come easy, but it did come to fruition.

Jacob lived in the land where his father had stayed, the land of Canaan.

This is the account of Jacob's family line.

Joseph, a young man of seventeen, was tending the flocks with his brothers, the sons of Bilhah and the sons of Zilpah, his father's wives, and he brought their father a bad report about them.

³ *Now Israel loved Joseph more than any of his other sons, because he had been born to him in his old age; and he made an ornate robe for him.* ⁴ *When his brothers saw that their father loved him more than any of them, they hated him and could not speak a kind word to him.*

⁵ *Joseph had a dream, and when he told it to his brothers, they hated him all the more.* ⁶ *He said to them, "Listen to this dream I had:* ⁷ *We were binding sheaves of grain out in the field when suddenly my sheaf rose and stood upright, while your sheaves gathered around mine and bowed down to it."*

⁸ *His brothers said to him, "Do you intend to reign over us? Will you actually rule us?" And they hated him all the more because of his dream and what he had said.*

⁹ *Then he had another dream, and he told it to his brothers. "Listen," he said, "I had another dream, and this time the sun and moon and eleven stars were bowing down to me."*

¹⁰ *When he told his father as well as his brothers, his father rebuked him and said, "What is this dream you had? Will*

your mother and I and your brothers actually come and bow down to the ground before you?" ¹¹ *His brothers were jealous of him, but his father kept the matter in mind.* **<u>Gen. 37:1-11</u>**

Encouraging Word: Faith pushes fear aside. Fear torments. We cannot give birth to His Promises, if we entertain fear. The Lord has a purpose for all of us. Many do not get to fulfill their God given purpose before leaving this earth.

That is unfortunate. You must get before the Lord and cry out to Him and ask him diligently, "what is my purpose?". Now, when He shows you that and He guides you toward it, do not look down at the water or you will drown.

You must look to the hills in which your help comes from. You must trust Him. To me this is so important, you must be willing to lose to gain. Because in Him to lose is to gain.

We want to hold on to 'stuff'. We think that 'stuff' is the most valuable treasure we have. It takes a Christian full of faith to know that our greatest valuable treasure is to know Christ in the pardoning of our sins and to take it to the next level, which is to trust Him beyond measure!

There are many people in marriages that do not trust their mate. They do not trust them as far as they can see them.

This Godly relationship must have a firm foundation. We must trust, then we can believe that whatever we ask in His name, He will provide.

I have learned through the laying on that floor that I can trust Christ for the impossible. I had to have that experience to know this without a shadow of a doubt. He taught me that no good thing will He withhold from me. He will supply me with all my needs.

We are surrounded by 'stuff' that we really do not need. If we ever get rid of the 'stuff', Christ will show us exactly what we need, and He will provide.

There will be some haters and some doubters. You will experience jealousy from those who decide not to walk by faith. Keep it moving.

He will send help our way in our time of trouble. He will make ways out of no ways. He will protect us from the snares of the enemy.

I had to learn all of that in order to become an effective businesswoman for Christ. When it did not always make sense to me, I still trusted.

Now that I am on the other side of nine years, it makes perfect sense. He knows our future well before we live it. With that being said, He knows what we must be put through to master what we will go through.

Glory to God! Step out, step up and go get your promise!

Chapter Five

FROM THE FLOOR TO THE FIRE

I THOUGHT MY greatest challenge was sleeping on the floor for nine months. This is not just a business for me, it is ministry.

I came into this business with no business experience. I came with years of healthcare knowledge, but no knowledge of how to run a business. It was a learn as you go.

After two years of running the business, I got a visit from the tax department. She mentioned to me that I owed payroll taxes. I did not know that I was supposed to pay payroll taxes.

By the time she came to visit me, I was $200,000+ in payroll tax debt. I paid my taxes on a yearly basis, but payroll taxes were different.

It was explained to me that the tax department had previously held classes for new business owners to enroll in to learn about this. Due to cutbacks, this training had been discontinued. She explained to me that 20-30 percent of new business owners are unaware of these taxes.

The company was making money and growing at a rapid pace. I had to continue to hire new staff. I had negotiated salaries without the knowledge of paying payroll taxes. I had charged my clients without the knowledge of the payroll tax information as well.

This meant that my ratios were off. I had a difficult time trying to implement paying the taxes prior to paying the employees.

Those taxes were running me approximately $50,000 a month. How do you incorporate this kind of money into your budget overnight?

I did not want to layoff. I kept trying to figure out ways to manage this. I had some sleepless nights, and I, at times felt overwhelmed and unqualified.

I still had other matters to handle as well as try to figure out a way to fix this monster. Many of my employees had come to me for personal counsel. I always made time for them, despite whatever I might be faced with.

I would close my office door and pray and encourage them. One of the precious things that I learned on the floor, was to lay aside my weight and help someone else get a breakthrough. I learned to take quiet moments to regroup. I learned to rest in the bosom of Jesus. I learned to lay my burdens down.

I heard a preacher say the other day that rest is a spiritual weapon. We do not know when to rest. When faced with great adversities, we must know when to rest so that we do not get spiritually burned out.

When things start to go awry, we tend to want to blame God. Of course, I went before the Lord and said, "You gave me this business, but You did not tell me about payroll taxes. How am I supposed to overcome this? Did {You really give me the vision to start this business"?

After we blame Him, we question what we once knew to be true. Where are those thoughts coming from? Who now wants to sabotage the blessing?

If a promise takes a turn, is it not still the promise? What did I learn on that floor? Yes, tenacity.

The tenacity to look the devil in the face and say, thou you slay me, yet I will trust. No, I am not blaming the devil for the back taxes, but I am holding him responsible for the thoughts that he wants to inundate me with.

All he needs is a truth and then he takes the truth and turns it into a lie. The truth is I owe taxes, the lie is that the Lord never led me to start the business.

I must take authority over the lie and trust the Lord in what is true. Because we serve Him, receive a vision or a promise from Him, does not mean that everything will flow freely and smoothly.

It does mean however, that He will equip us to fight and sustain our faith even during hardships and disappointments.

I started this business with $0 dollars and without a cushion. The Lord knew I had $0 when He gave me the promise.

This business was not built on dollars, it was built on faith. Now nine years after, I see that it was faith that carried me through the nine years. There was a lesson to be learned in that.

Did I make errors along the way? Yes indeed. My back has been up against the wall, embedded in the wall and at times a full dent in the wall, but I did not crumble.

I always thought that this business was ministry for others, but it has been my greatest ministry for myself.

The Lord equipped me while lying on the floor, how to endure and persevere while under character assassination. I had some powerful prayer warriors in my corner, encouraging me along the way.

My goal is to leave an inheritance to my children's children. Break the back of poverty off our lives. We have struggled long enough. That kind of goal does not come without a battle.

I can imagine what Joseph must have felt. He was given the vision to prevent a famine in his family's life and he was hated and despised for it.

When the Lord uses us to make a major change in our life that will also affect so many others, there is a battle that we must endure.

We must hold fast to the vision and gird ourselves up for the battle. So, I accepted the challenge and was ready to do whatever I could to right this wrong.

The first step was to get a good tax attorney to represent me and the business and find a way to resolve this matter.

I felt good in my spirit that it would all work to the good because I had kept my integrity intact and never tried to cut any corners or cheat the system in any way.

This was an honest but costly error on my behalf. As long as we live in this world, we are going to make mistakes. How the mistake is concluded is what makes the difference. We should first accept that we made a mistake, then correct it and learn from it. Make it a lifetime goal not to make the same mistake twice.

I cannot say that it will not be the case, but to strive for perfection going forward is not a bad goal to try to accomplish!

I made up my mind that instead of having ungodly thoughts, I would focus on the One who could help me through this situation. No one to blame, but a lesson to learn.

I started seeking counsel from those who are smarter than myself. I did this through prayer. I asked the Lord to put those in my pathway who would be able to provide me with good insight and direction. He did exactly what I requested in prayer.

I would meet with some of the most brilliant, successful women and they helped me spiritually, financially, personally, and well as emotionally get through this debacle.

It is like He strategically put them all in place. I genuinely love the Lord with all my heart and soul. He never leaves or forsakes us.

If I kept focusing on how this could happen, then I would not have been able to see what was happening and that was that He was placing people in my life that would teach me and help guide me into becoming a successful Christian businesswoman.

So glad I had an ear to hear what the spirit of the Lord was saying. During those challenging days I would go to noon day prayer on Tuesdays and Thursdays and my First Lady would pray for me and the business and rebuke the hands of the enemy.

The power of agreement is a force to be reckoned! Those agreement sessions would elevate my faith another notch.

As many as the Lord brought in my life that was for me, the enemy brought his army in that would be against me.

I will leave that right there and conclude that there be more for me, than against me. Hallelujah!!!

Victory truly belongs to God's people and for those who have an ear to hear.

Look at the Hebrew boys, who refused to bow down to other gods and how the Son of God showed up on their behalf:

13 Furious with rage, Nebuchadnezzar summoned Shadrach, Meshach and Abednego. So. these men were brought before the king, 14 and Nebuchadnezzar said to them, "Is it true, Shadrach, Meshach and Abednego, that you do not serve my gods or worship the image of gold I have set up? 15 Now when you hear the sound of the horn, flute, zither, lyre, harp, pipe and all kinds of music, if you are ready to fall down and worship the image I made, very good. But if you do not worship it, you will be thrown immediately into a blazing furnace. Then what god will be able to rescue you from my hand?"

¹⁶ Shadrach, Meshach and Abednego replied to him, "King Nebuchadnezzar, we do not need to defend ourselves before you in this matter. ¹⁷ If we are thrown into the blazing furnace, the, God we serve is able to deliver us from it, and he will deliver us] from Your Majesty's hand. ¹⁸ But even if he does not, we want you to know, Your Majesty, that we will not serve your gods or worship the image of gold you have set up."

¹⁹ Then Nebuchadnezzar was furious with Shadrach, Meshach and Abednego, and his attitude toward them changed. He ordered the furnace heated seven times hotter than usual ²⁰ and commanded some of the strongest soldiers in his army to tie up Shadrach, Meshach and Abednego and throw them into the blazing furnace. ²¹ So these men, wearing their robes, trousers, turbans and other clothes, were bound and thrown into the blazing furnace. ²² The king's command was so urgent and the furnace so hot that the flames of the fire killed the soldiers who took up Shadrach, Meshach and Abednego, ²³ and these three men, firmly tied, fell into the blazing furnace.

²⁴ Then King Nebuchadnezzar leaped to his feet in amazement and asked his advisers, "Weren't there three men that we tied up and threw into the fire?"

They replied, "Certainly, Your Majesty."

^{25} He said, "Look! I see four men walking around in the fire, unbound and unharmed, and the fourth looks like a son of the gods." Daniel 3:13-25

Encouraging Word: I do not care what you are faced with, He is more than able to bring you out. Walking out in faith does not mean it will be a perfect journey, however, it does solidify that He will be with you every step of the way.

The enemy talks loud to discourage, but the spirit of the Lord speaks volume to every situation and shuts the mouth of the enemy every time.

We must make sure we prevent getting sidetracked and not get off the journey of our promise. Obstacles will present themselves to make it look like it will fail, but I encourage you on today that it will not fail.

Remember that the Lord is a *restorer, redeemer, rescuer,* and He *reaffirms.* Whenever you begin to question the promise, take it to prayer and always be reminded of these (4) R's.

If you waiver in your belief, acknowledge that you did, refocus and continue your journey to your path of promise.

Do not beat yourself up, we all fall short to the glory of God. The key is to be able to discern what is true and recognize what plot is being planned against you. Do not fall victim to the plot but press toward the mark of the high calling which is the destiny to your promise.

We have a work to do and the Lord has something special for you to accomplish in this lifetime that will be a benefit to His kingdom.

We often wonder is there more to just being born to die and the question is yes. The goal is to find what you were destined to fulfill, and you can only find out by being in true communion with Christ through the Holy Spirit.

What are you waiting for, there is a promise for you to fulfill – get busy!!

Chapter Six

Take This Cup

After working out various payment plans with the tax department, I would still find myself not able to keep up with paying toward the back balance as well as paying for the current payroll taxes.

At any given time, I could look in the business accounts and see that all the money was withdrawn by the tax department.

These surprising deductions usually took place a day before or on payday. With no money, I still had to manage to pay seventy-five employees.

An employee who has worked is required to get paid, whether there is money or not. As the President it was my duty to make this legally happen.

There were days when I had to have the staff wait until a day or two to get paid. I needed time to secure the funds through other legal means.

There were times that I would close my office door and just fall on my knees and cry out to the Lord to make a way. Sometimes I could only groan. I thought that this cross was way too much for me to bare.

I had a caring staff of Managers that would work along with me to find the means to meet the payroll, but this was solely on me. It was my responsibility and I carried it into the night.

I never laid down unpeacefully. Once I laid my head on my pillow, I went to sleep trusting that the Lord would provide.

There were several times when the tax department told me that they would not take any monies and my account would show contrary to their spoken word. They would tell my tax attorney that the system inadvertently took the money by 'accident', however, they could not reverse it because I did indeed owe.

Despite the unforeseen 'accident', I had a payroll to meet. When I look back at that devastating period of my life, I can honestly say that it was nothing but the grace of

God that the payroll was met and that I remained in my right mind!

I did not let the circumstances keep me from being His witness. I continued to encourage the staff that needed to hear a Word from the Lord. No way did the Lord allow this situation to kill my character and who He called me to be.

I saw the plot very clearly and declared that I would not succumb to the set up.

Oftentimes, we say that the Pastors children are the ones who are the most wayward. We gossip about it; we even make jokes concerning it.

Did you ever spiritually ask and seek the Lord on this issue? I understand why the bible says to keep your leaders and their family in prayer.

While a Pastor is teaching and preaching your soul free, the enemy is constantly attacking them and their family. If he can distract the head, he can crumble the entire body.

The attack is greater than you realize. If he can discredit the Pastor or any of his family members, he can convince the flock or a potential soul, that this life is not worth living. Spiritual warfare is very much real.

Instead of judging your leaders and their children, continue to pray for them, so that you may be fed the unadulterated Word of God. I am not talking about serving a Pastor that is living a life full of sin and not living what he is preaching.

I am talking about the Pastor who is being bombarded with health issues, children are constantly under attack, wife is overwhelmed with the grief because of the circumstances surrounding her family.

There is a suffering that comes with righteous living. It is a shear discouraging hit that wants to keep the believer out of place.

When you try to live and do right, it can open a door of confusion to keep you off balance. But if you keep doing what you are doing, it shall pass, and the Lord will get the glory!

I start recognizing these 'accidents' for what they truly were. All I could do was get on my knees and say, "Lord, you know all, and you see all, please protect your servant from the unseen forces".

It had been suggested to me for several years to close the business because there was no way that I could rebound from this.

My tax attorney kept advising me to strongly consider it because she never saw the tax department come at a business so aggressively and have so many 'accidents' occur that was out of their hands.

I kept on fighting for what I felt was right and that was to keep the business open and believe the Lord's word, that the door He opens no man can shut.

The tax department continued to get more aggressive as time went on. The more aggressive they became, the more I saw the hands of the Lord at work in my life.

I had to do some laying off to try to compensate for the losses the business had incurred. I was cutting down the payroll expenses so that I could meet the needs of the tax department.

I was sitting at my desk one morning and I heard the Holy Spirit very clearly say to me, "it's time to shut this aspect of the business down". I cannot explain it, but a peaceful calm came over me and I said, "ok Lord, if you say so". He said, "I need you to trust me as I guide you through this". Again, I said, "ok Lord, I will".

I agreed with the tax department that it was time to close out the business as they had previously suggested.

We had to break down the business. We transferred all 215 clients to different agencies, and we found the 55+ employees job opportunities with other agencies.

I felt a calming peace that I did not owe any employees money and that each one had another job opportunity awaiting them.

I had to show the tax department that the business had been dissolved as requested. I then sat in my office space and wondered what the next step for my life would be. I thought about Jesus before He went to the cross. He first went to the Garden of Gethsemane to pray:

[40] On reaching the place, he said to them, "Pray that you will not fall into temptation." [41] He withdrew about a stone's throw beyond them, knelt down and prayed, [42] "Father, if you are willing, take this cup from me; yet not my will, but yours be done." [43] An angel from heaven appeared to him and strengthened him. [44] And being in

anguish, he prayed more earnestly, and his sweat was like drops of blood falling to the ground. **Luke 22:40-44**

For a moment, the human side of Jesus was asking the Father to take the cup, perhaps it was too much to bear. Although He knew the promise had to be fulfilled, for a second it became an overwhelming thought. It was then that the Father brought an angel to come and strengthen Him and He prayed in anguish and more earnestly.

He gave His pain to the Father in the garden that is what the anguish was about. There are some things we cannot bare alone. After the pain is released, we can pray more earnestly.

I accepted the task ahead of me once I gave my pain over to the Lord. I cried loud and spared not. I waited for further instructions from the Holy Spirit.

The owner of the office space where I was leasing agreed that I could remain in the office as I planned for my future.

It was then that the Lord instructed me on the new name for my business. I would restart the business with a clean slate. The doors never closed! The Lord is true to His Word. I thank Him for the favor that was extended to me.

Encouraging Word: His grace is truly sufficient! The promise was not aborted. I trusted the Lord and I adhered to His direction and He did not steer me wrong.

Has this encouraged you in anyway? I pray so. I do not mind sharing my most trying times with the world. It was something I promised the Lord I would do from the day I received His precious Holy Spirit.

You see, when He brings us out of a situation that was meant to defeat us, we MUST tell it. Some will analyze this ordeal and point out my faults, and that is alright. But if you stay focused on how I should have handled the circumstance, you will miss the move of the Holy Spirit.

I will be the first to say that I errored, and that there are consequences for not paying your taxes. I fully get that. It is some of the unseen actions that the Lord had to step in and bring to light, to cover and protect me from.

The ability to discern is a powerful tool for the believer. Everything that appears to be right and in line may not always be that way.

Can I let you in on a secret? Everyone is not rooting for your success. Oops, I said it. Especially if you came from the back to the front, from the lower man on the totem pole to the upper echelon. People can tend to put you on their level of success. They do not mind you obtaining some success, but not too much.

Those thoughts get into the airwaves and they pick up legs and arms and they get to work on trying to make those thoughts a truth.

Then there are angels dispatched to make sure that the plans and the promises that the Lord has for you come to full fruition. It is a spiritual battle that we are usually oblivious to.

However, if you are filled with the Holy Spirit, the battle is now within your radar and you pick up these negative thoughts and you begin to see the angels at work on your behalf.

What is a striving person to do? Stay focus on the journey and keep it moving for His glory! Keep your spiritual ear open and your spirit man alert.

All I hear right now is the song that says: We got the victory. Sweet, sweet, victory.

Every morning that I enter my office suite, I thank the Lord for rescuing me. He is a redeemer!

Chapter Seven

HIS PROMISE IS GREATER THAN THE PLOT!

I REALIZE THAT I have made it by the grace of God. He instructed me to pack my bags and follow Him. I was obedient, and I did so, and I did not look back.

I am blessed to say that my children are doing well. I am blessed with four beautiful grandchildren who bring me so much joy.

I know that the Lord wants to break the spirit of lack in the generations that follow me, and He chose me to lay that foundation.

He broke me to bless me. When I sold all that I had and resorted to sleeping on the floor in my office, there was a breaking that took place.

He did not break my spirit; He broke my way of thinking. He broke my way of operating. He broke my way of handling matters. He broke the spirit of lack over my family.

When I rose from the floor, I rose with a new determination. I was determined to endure whatever hardship that had to come to birth the newness into my children and my children's children.

When I embrace them, it is a reward for the brokenness I had to encounter. It built strength and character in me.

I always say that our lives are like a puzzle. All pieces are needed to bring the picture to completion.

The joyful times, the sorrowful times, the disappointing times, the fulfilling times are all a part of our completion.

I learned that there are precious jewels buried in the valleys of our lives. The mountains formed in our life should make our foundation rock solid! We can use those mountains to climb to higher heights and deeper depths in faith.

When we are weak, He makes us strong. If you come across a situation in your life that seems impossible to accomplish, remember, that is the very assignment that is meant to bring your faith to the next level.

If you love good challenges, then remain in salvation and you will never get bored. We are taught to be overcomers. To overcome, you must be faced with something.

You have people who live what seems to be perfectly planned lives and they cannot fathom going through half of what others may encounter.

They believe to serve God you have to go through unnecessary suffering and pain. What they do not realize is that the suffering you encounter for righteous sake, is so that you can learn to endure and not be demolished by a raving storm.

If their perfect life is interrupted by an 'issue' of life, it becomes totally unbearable. The Lord teaches His people how to endure hardship and build character from it.

We are fooling ourselves if we believe we can live this life minus suffering. There is self-inflicted suffering and then there is the suffering that comes simply because you decided to live for Jesus. However, that suffering comes with rewards. He that suffers with Him shall reign with Him.

I am just overly grateful that the pressure that was put on me to cause me to collapse did not accomplish what it was set out to do. I thank God that the Lord saw fit to cover and protect me.

I vowed to the Lord that I would avail myself to Him even the more. If you ever recovered from a circumstance that was formed to take you out, and you survived it, you can fully relate to what I am saying.

It causes you to run with more fervor. It reveals Christ to you in a more real and powerful way.

What I had to go through to break a generational curse, may not be the way another might have to go through.

He deals with us all in different ways. However, His word is true, and it can apply itself to all who believe.

In other words, the formula is the same. His way of escape is the same. His love is the same. What He does for one, He will do for another. If we just believe.

Not too many people can withstand the tactics of the tax department. It turned from collecting their money, to taking me down.

I remember one day agents drove to my house, looked through my windows and then banged on my door. When my daughter answered, they were in awe to see that I still resided there.

Upset by seeing that I had not lost everything, they came to my office next. It baffled them that I was still there and had established my new business.

They even made phone calls to see how I was able to remain there after they had taken all my money. They even inquired as to why I wasn't evicted.

Those 'mistakes' of taking money in error were meant to leave me penniless, homeless and hopeless. But the Lord Jesus Christ said, not so!

I remember my last phone call from them. It was their last opportunity to 'break me'. It started off by asking me about information concerning the new company. They wanted to make sure I did not have the same clients and employees from the previous company. These questions were very legit to ask.

The conversation began to take a turn. Instead of questioning the setup of the new company, the agent began to say that nothing I touch would prosper and I would fail at trying to grow the new business. He further said that I should just give up and count my losses. This is when

I realized that my matter had changed players. It was no longer the agent and I; it was a demonic force from a high place, angry that I had not succumb to all the other tactics.

My lawyer was on the phone with me and she said, "this is way over the top. I have never heard an agent disrespect a business owner in this manner".

I must admit that it was the most painful encounter that I have ever experienced. The Lord that I serve held my hand every step of the way.

Owing the taxes was my issue, how it was handled, became the Lord's battle!

Encouraging Word: When the Word of the Lord says that He will give you double for your trouble; I can honestly say I know this to be true. This business will be opened in many states.

For every great promise there is a plot set against it. Truly what the enemy means for our harm, the Lord will turn it for our good.

He made me a promise, and He wanted to know would I stand firm on the promise and watch the salvation of the Lord.

Although the storms raged and the winds blew, our Lord showed me how to endure.

The enemy will paint a picture of destruction and he will use whatever vessel is available to try to demolish the promise.

The enemy comes with an element of truth. The truth was that I owed taxes and arrangements were made to pay them off. Monies were constantly taken out of my account by 'accident' which made the ability to keep the arrangements impossible.

The plot had many purposes, which I pointed out. Its desire was to leave me penniless, homeless, and hopeless.

Why? I am glad you wondered. I have been penniless, homeless, and hopeless and the Lord had promised me with this business, I would not encounter these defeats again. Word got out to the enemy and he tried to use the tax issue to circumvent the plan of the Lord.

They had stopped focusing on collecting the debt, to just destroying me. I was not to the place with them to start retrieving my assets. They were perplexed about how I was able to maintain while they were in the process of assuming all my money.

The bible says in, **Romans 5:3-5** *Not only so but we also glory in our sufferings, because we know that suffering produces perseverance, 4perservance character and character hope. 5And hope does not put us to shame, because God's love has been poured out into our hearts through the Holy Spirit, who has been given to us.*

He taught me through all of this, to still love and not to be angry or bitter toward those who bring intentional targeted pain my way.

I don't care what you are facing, don't let fear stop you, instead let it be your motivator.

<u>**Courageous means**</u> the state or quality of mind or spirit that enables one to face danger with confidence and resolution, bravery, and valor.

<u>**Fear means**</u> – expectation of danger, pain and disaster.

<u>**Faith means**</u> according to Hebrews 11:1 Now Faith is confidence in what we hope for and assurance about what we do not see.

If the Lord promised it to you, He will equip you for the task. I do not care how strong one is in their faith, with new ground, new territory and a new level in your walk, you will face fear head on. Courageous fear gives us the ability to face our fear, danger and pain with confidence that the Lord will cover and shield us from the plot that will try to discourage and keep us from obtaining our spiritual goals. That kind of courage is faith.

God bless you!

Chapter Eight

Closing Prayer

Lord, we thank you for Who you are. I do pray in Your mighty name that there is something said in this book that will encourage someone to step out and walk into their divine purpose.

I pray that the Holy Spirit will guide and direct every decision they make. Speak to their spirit and dismantle every plot and deception that the enemy will try to bring their way.

Lord continue to show us how we can trust and depend on you for all things. Remove any fear that may try to entangle us into believing that we cannot achieve the things that have been promised to us.

Let faith walk in our lives like never before. Let us not just quote the Word but be doers of the Word of God.

Lord, let us truly know that nothing is impossible for those who believe.

Your people of God are the extensions of you on this earth. You deserve to have soldiers who will stand on the front line and represent the authority that you have given them.

In times like these, you need your people to walk in full authority so that you may get the glory!

For us to do this, we must walk in our divine purpose and authority. My fervent prayer is that you will reveal purpose!

If our will for our life does not line up with the will you have, then speak to us and show us Lord.

We desire to be pleasing unto you. It is so easy to get caught up on what the world has determined for our destiny, that we omit to seek the Lord's face when it comes to key decisions.

Today, we seek your face. Let your perfect will be done so that you may be pleased with your servants.

No matter what we face, you are greater, and you know best. Do not let the spirit of fear silence our heart from hearing from you.

Closing Prayer

We come boldly to the throne room of grace with our petition and supplications. We know that greater is in us, than he that is in the world.

In Jesus Name, Amen!

About the Author:

Ms. Thigpen is the author of "He Hears our Prayers".

She is an Associate Pastor/Evangelist/Author/Entrepreneur.

She is the mother of two and has four wonderful, anointed and appointed grandbabies.

She is married to the awesome, anointed Bishop George W. Thigpen and they enjoy spending time with family and operating in ministry together.

Together, her and her Husband are working on a third book titled, 'Our Spiritual Battle with Covid-19'.

She boldly walks by faith and not by sight.

www.ingramcontent.com/pod-product-compliance
Ingram Content Group UK Ltd.
Pitfield, Milton Keynes, MK11 3LW, UK
UKHW041950230426
12048UKWH00008B/243